WHY I COULDN'T FIGHT

by Lloy A. Kniss

 **CHRISTIAN LIGHT PUBLICATIONS**
Harrisonburg, Va. 22801

Christian Light Publications, Inc.
Harrisonburg, Virginia 22801-1212
© 1994 by Christian Light Publications, Inc.
All rights reserved. Published 1994
Printed in the United States of America

09 08 07 06 05 04 03 02 01 00   9 8 7 6 5

ISBN 0-87813-507-3
Linthographed in U.S.A.

Foreword

My former booklet entitled, "I Couldn't Fight," is only an account of some actions and reactions arising from deep convictions born in me from my first-hand faith. This faith came from my understanding of God's Word, under the guidance of the Holy Spirit.

I feel indebted to the readers of that booklet to explain more about the faith and convictions behind those actions and reactions, for I would have them experience the same spiritual satisfactions and security I feel because of what God has done and is doing for me. This then is my first reason for this writing.

I am also deeply concerned about the change in the general attitude of many people toward the doctrine of nonresistance. Nonresistance is a New Testament discipline for believers; it is necessary for a rounded-out Christian life. It applies to the saints, or disciples of Christ. I have, on the other hand, never felt that we are to teach it to society in general in an effort to reform that society and so consider ourselves as peacemakers in the world. This, however, seems to be the trend among many of our brethren and sisters today. I do not believe that nonresistance is something we use to patch up our battered society, but it is intended to beautify and purify Christian people so their witness might be more effective in the salvation of souls. This is another reason for my writing this present booklet.

Some people dislike the term nonresistance. The expression, "peaceful living," might be more positive, but the term "pacifism" carries an undesirable connotation. Some use the term "nonviolence." This is much weaker than "nonresistance." Nonresistance includes such phases as "not going to law" and "the second mile." "Nonviolence" would involve only such acts as killing, murder, maiming, and fighting—those things which would destroy or injure by great force or wild passion. Also, nonviolence, which is a comparatively recent term, is closely related to noncooperation, and civil disobedience which often provoke violence. We would do well to keep the term "nonresistance," for it covers well all the Biblical phases of this subject.

There is also among some folks too much anti-government or anti-American feeling. It is true that the church and the state are separate entities. Without condoning things that are wrong about our country or our rulers, we can honor and respect them as Christ taught us to do. We respect rulers as rulers. It is not our role to judge and classify officials honoring only those we think are good. Fault-finding comes too easily for some of us.

It is not our role as Christians to insist, or even suggest, that government officers operate by Christian principles.

In this writing I have let the Bible be its own

interpreter, depending on the Holy Spirit to illumine the Word. This, along with my observations of the confused thinking among our people about this subject, has given me the convictions I have expressed.

My prayer in presenting this brief treatise is that it may help some of our own young people to know the reasons for their faith and that it may also help the youth of various other denominations who are searching for light in the matter of nonresistance.

Lloy A. Kniss

Contents

Foreword

Introduction 7

Chapter I, The Subject 9

Chapter II, My Background 14

Chapter III, Our Present Situation 18

Chapter IV, Biblical Reasons for
    Nonresistance 21

Chapter V, Additional Reasons 28

Chapter VI, Related Involvements 36

Chapter VII, Related Questions 61

Introduction

"Why I Couldn't Fight" is more than a catchy title for a book. It involves an issue deserving logical answers from the Bible. Lloy A. Kniss, a man of broad and varied experiences as school teacher, foreign missionary, minister and bishop, has in a most interesting and effective manner, given the answers.

Having worked with the author, as a pastor under his supervision, for about twenty years, I have found him to be a real "peacemaker" with an unusual working knowledge of the Bible. He has rightly warned against participation in various forms of popular worldly pacifism, none of which are in line with New Testament Christianity. Of equal importance is his emphasis on the difference in God's rules for His people under the Old Testament covenant and those for the Christian Church as found in the New Testament. The emphasis on a day-by-day practice of peace and nonresistance on the part of all Christians is of great importance. It is entirely in line with God's instructions for the life and conduct of the Christian Church as revealed in the New Testament.

It is my sincere prayer that many will read this book prayerfully and come to a more Biblical understanding and practice in a very important phase of Christian living in this New Testament Church age. —Ray Shenk

To the Intelligence Officer

1 The Subject

"Why can't you fight?" These words came "at me" clothed in the deep, gruff voice of a portly intelligence officer seated behind his large desk.

It was a mild 1918 winter morning in Camp Greenleaf, at Fort Oglethorpe, Georgia. The corporal of our C.O. detachment told me I was called to appear before the Intelligence Officer. I quickly got ready to go. A special guard with a bayonet attached to his rifle was instructed to march me to the place which was about two miles from our tents. He walked behind me with his gun in both hands pointed at my back, the bayonet all but touching me. This gave the appearance of a dangerous person being marched down the road. I knew the guard had no ill will toward me. I can imagine he probably felt embarrassed, for he knew I would not try to run away. He was under orders from his superior. We didn't talk together except when he told me where to turn.

We finally arrived and I was ushered into the office.

"What do you want here?" the deep, gruff voice asked me from the other side of the desk.

"Sir, I don't know, but I was told you called for me."

He scowled and asked roughly, "Why can't you fight?" I answered his question, but he was not interested in my answer. He spoke very roughly and asked me, "Don't you ever fight?"

"No, Sir."

"I don't believe you!"

"Sir, I didn't say that I never fought. I said I don't fight."

"Tell me, when did you fight?"

"When I was a boy I fought with my brothers and with my schoolmates at times. But, Sir, I don't fight now."

"Do you ever tell lies?"

"No, Sir, I do not."

"You're telling one right now."

"Sir, I didn't say I never told lies. I only said I don't tell lies."

That settled that, but this kind of conversation went on for quite some time. Seemingly, he tried to make me angry so that I would answer sharply or show anger in some other way.

"What we ought to do with fellows like you is back you up against that wall and blow your little brain out with a shotgun."

I did not respond unless there was something in my facial expression of which I was not aware. I know there was no anger in my heart, but there was, I admit, some fear.

The officer wrote on a sheet of paper every time I replied to one of his many questions. Disgustedly he gave the paper a shove as though he wanted to push it out of his way in order to get up from his chair. He arose and said, "Wait here till I come back."

It happened that the paper slid close enough that I could have read it, but at once something told me not to read it or even look at it. I didn't.

After about ten minutes the officer returned and sat down. He pulled the paper back to himself. Then he started all over, in an angry mood grueling me with the same kind of questions as before. While he was doing it the second time, he kept looking at the paper. I was glad I had not read it. I think it was a trap.

Suddenly his countenance changed, and his voice changed to a soft, kind, warm tone. "Your government," he said, "has found you worthy to be furloughed out on a farm instead of spending your time here in camp." He spoke very kindly to me like a father talking to a son he loved. It seemed he loved me, in a certain sense. He told me I would be on a farm in about two weeks, and then he gave me very good advice on how to conduct myself in that community. He said I would be watched by people who would report back to camp.

"Now you may go again, and I wish you a good time on that farm."

"Thank you, Sir." I started back to my tent, again walking ahead of the guard. When I went to the office, the road was rough and hard. However, walking back was much easier; I was "walking on air."

My reply to his question, "Why can't you fight?" was only a vain effort to be specific, but I tried to be courteous. If I had been less frightened and had given him a full explanation, he probably would have had neither time nor patience to listen to it all. He wasn't really interested in a clear answer as to my reason for not being able to fight. He was only reprimanding me for failing to cooperate with the officers in the various activities of this army camp.

I was also unable to state my reasons as clearly at that time as I can state them now, fifty-five years later. Most of the reasons were in my mind then, but I couldn't fully verbalize them.

For this writing I am assuming that the question, "Why can't you fight?" is being asked in sincerity and not as a reprimand.

They Don't Add Up

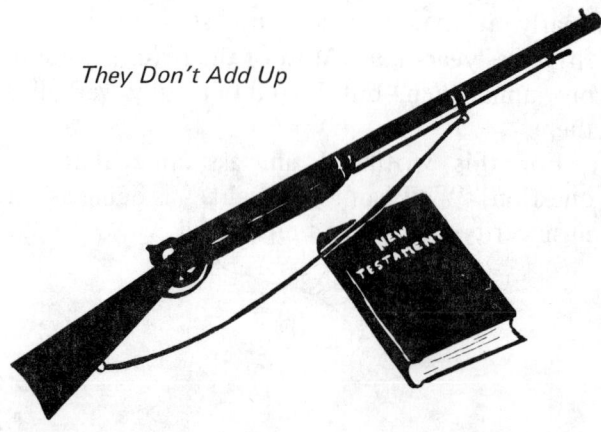

2 My Background

When I was a boy, probably about ten, it was fully evident that I had inherited a good share of "fight" from my ancestors. I say evident, because I had three brothers and some schoolmates, equally aggressive, with whom I occasionally clashed in carnal ways.

The "fight" I had was really an asset in meeting the struggles of life. But evil came from it when I did not control my passions. The net results of not properly dealing with my natural instincts were a troubled, insecure inner life and the realization that to really live I needed help beyond my own self.

I yielded my life to Christ when I was eleven. The peace I began to experience then is still a reassuring memory after sixty years. But I had to learn and apply various disciplines needed for further understanding and growth in the Christian life.

The first test I faced after yielding myself to Christ was the next day in school.

There was a girl in our school (whom I will call June), who was considerably oversize. She was somewhat older than I and was one of the mother-type girls, usually found in one-room schools, to whom the smaller children go for comfort and help. June was kind-natured, and she and I had always respected each other.

When I went to school the morning after my commitment, she came right away. "I hear now you want to be a 'goodie goodie,' " she laughed. She was a teenager and not a Christian, but had always been very nice to me before. This affected me very much, but it helped to prepare me for later life when opposition was more severe.

When I was growing up, I was exposed to a variety of alternatives as standards for my life. The general attitude of people was that a person who would not fight for his rights was a weakling, and one who refused to fight for his country was guilty of sin. Then there were the peace churches that taught that war is wrong, and some churches that taught that some wars

15

are wrong. My ancestors and relatives on my father's side were all Lutheran, and patriotism was a strong tradition with them. My mother and her side of my relatives were Mennonite; for them war was wrong.

My father's two uncles were soldiers in the Civil War. My paternal grandparents and others in the family often talked of these two uncles in highly respectful terms. My father had in his possession a muzzle-loading gun which one of his uncles had used in the war. He occasionally got out this gun and showed it to visitors who came to our house.

The history books and other textbooks in our school, as well as our teachers, continually glorified soldiers who fought well and were highly honored in various ways.

From my mother and later from the church of my choice, which was also Mennonite, I received the teaching that it is wrong for Christians to kill people regardless of circumstances. This, of course, was in line with what my Christian experience seemed to say was right. While I was still a teenager, my father also became a Mennonite and embraced the same ideals. Before my father became a Mennonite, we as a family attended the Lutheran and Mennonite churches alternately. There were many things in my father's church which appealed to me, but by God's providence I embraced biblical faith with regard to war—nonresistance to evil (Matthew

5:39). This, of course, refers to carnal resistance.

As I remember, I never thought a nonresistant life was the weak, spineless kind of life that many of my peers thought it was.

While I was in camp during World War I, the officers often attributed my stand against war to the way I was brought up. It was not only my bringing up, but my own conviction received from the Bible. I remember keenly my early regard for the Bible as the Word of God, which was taught by my parents and my pastor. God gave me this conviction through the Word and the Holy Spirit. I was free to follow the early influence of my father and his church and my schoolteachers, or the teachings of the Mennonite Church. With these alternatives from which to choose, my decision was not a passive yielding to my early environment, but was made according to my understanding of God's will.

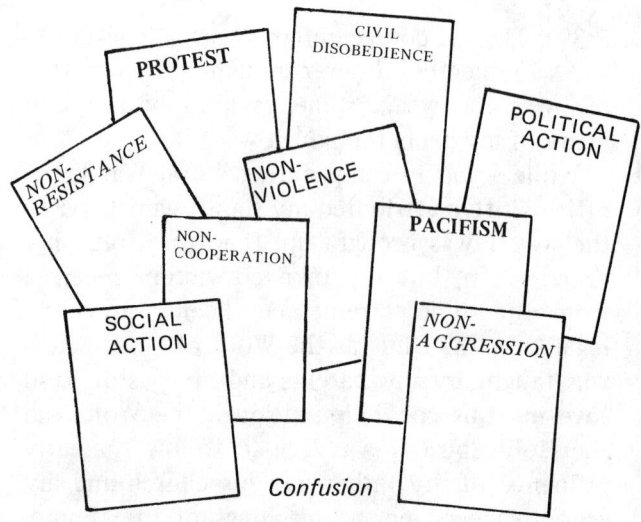

Confusion

3 Our Present Situation

Confusion among peace-loving people today is threatening our position. (Confusion and peace are not good partners. To connect them sounds like a paradox.) Differences of opinion and different bases for peace have caused this confusion.

There are differences in belief and also in practice. Sometimes it is only a difference in the use or connotation of terms.

Biblical nonresistance and popular pacifism are mostly miles apart. Some other forms of belief and practice related to pacifism are:

nonviolence, nonaggression, noncooperation, civil disobedience, protests, and political action. All these confuse the minds of our young people.

I want to discuss New Testament nonresistance rather than these other practices because I think from the Bible point of view it is the only valid practice for the Christian.

Some people object to using such a negative term as nonresistance, but it is taken from the Bible and we will consider it valid. We are told not to resist evil (Matt. 5:39). What is so very bad about using negative terms anyway? The words "not" and "do not" are frequently used in the Bible. If some modern students had written or edited the ten commandments, they likely would have written "Thou shalt tell the truth," instead of "Thou shalt not bear false witness." If it were written that way, surely some would say, "I do tell the truth—when it suits!" It is much better as it is, so I will continue to say "nonresistance" and be honest.

Even among those who agree that nonresistance is the only valid position, a few disagree as to the interpretation and the application of the principle.

Some feel they can perform noncombatant army service. Some are willing to support a war by money donations or loans. Some readily manipulate their vocations or businesses to benefit by higher prices of certain products in time of war. Some would be willing to accept employment in factories which make munitions or weapons and the like.

One day in camp my lieutenant handed me a clipping from a certain church paper. The article was written by a minister in another branch of the Mennonite church. This lieutenant seemed to gloat over the prospect that, as he thought, he could prove to me that I was wrong in my stand, and that I was suffering uselessly. The minister recommended to his young men (and all others) that they sign up for the noncombatant service in the army. This was in the first world war. The differences among us today are even more subtle than that.

Be Not Unequally Yoked with Unbelievers

4 Biblical Reasons for Nonresistance

There are two basic reasons in the New Testament why it is wrong for a Christian to resist evil or to kill.

First, "Separation from the world." The opposition I experienced from some of my neighbors and schoolmates who were not Christians lined up with this concept. This did not make me feel superior over others, but it gave me poise and security, knowing that I had a place in the world even though I was not a part of it. This concept is considered by Bible students as a part of Christian doctrine. When Jesus prayed for us in John 17:15, He said, "I pray not that thou shouldest take them out of the world, but that thou shouldest keep them from the evil."

One evening when I was still new in camp, we got orders to come out of our tents and follow the lieutenant. He led us to a comfortable spot in the edge of the woods to lecture to us. I was the lone C.O., but wasn't noticed so much yet by the others; we were all new, young boys from all walks of life. If I had known what we were going for, I might have refused to go to this lecture which was intended to make better soldiers out of the rookies in our company.

The lieutenant began lecturing to us in an effort to harden us against everything that pertained to home, church, or God. To me it was almost unbelievable that an official in authority over several hundred young men could talk the way he did. The whole lecture was a torrent of smut, vulgarity, obscenity, and blasphemy against everything sacred—filthy jokes about mothers, teachers, preachers; blasphemies against God and Christ; obscene jokes about sex and missing nothing that could be utilized to deprave the minds of these young men.

The question, "What fellowship hath righteousness with unrighteousness?" is surely pertinent.

"My kingdom is not of this world," Jesus said in John 18:36. He continued: "If my kingdom were of this world, then would my servants fight, that I should not be delivered to the Jews: but now is my kingdom not from hence." This teaching of Jesus, backed by His exemplary attitude when He approached the cross, certainly is the guide for our life.

This principle of nonretaliation, or nonresistance, or nonkilling of humans, applies not only to war. In my mind it is just as sinful to be a quarrelsome neighbor or a person who causes church troubles, as it is to take part in war. That there is a difference between Christians and non-Christians is too obvious for debate.

To expect civil officers to live and rule by the principle of love in all situations would be futile. In some situations it can be done, but not always. Sometimes even physical force must be employed to survive, and to them survival is essential. Government officers must ultimately employ force, even with carnal weapons. Rom. 13:4 says about the civil ruler, "He beareth not the sword in vain." Christians are not to use the sword. Their work in the world is different from that of civil officers.

The Christian way of life is unique in being nonresistant. Of all the other religions in the world, there is none whose founder established his leadership as Christ did, by dying and rising again after three days. A number of other founders established their leadership by killing their enemies.

It is human nature to strike back, but it is not natural for Christians with the new nature to strike back. This clearly points up that there are two kingdoms which are separate. Paul writes, by Holy Spirit inspiration, to the Corinthian Christians, "Be ye not unequally yoked together with unbelievers: for what fellowship hath righteousness with unrighteousness? and what communion hath light with darkness? And what concord hath Christ with Belial? or what part hath he that believeth with an infidel? And what agreement hath the temple of God with idols? for ye are the temple of the living God; as God hath said, I will dwell in them, and walk in them; and I will be their God, and they shall be my people. Wherefore come out from among them, and be ye separate, saith the Lord, and touch not the unclean thing. . ." (II Cor. 6:14-17).

When I was in camp in 1918, the officers in essence, continually tried to get me to be a part of the army. They kept saying, "You won't need to kill anyone, you can work in the noncombatant division." They were willing for me to do or not to do certain things, but they wanted me to be identified as part of the army.

One of the principal ways I could have shown my identity with the army was to wear the army uniform. They asked me to wear it, and I refused. One evening a lieutenant came to my tent and talked very kindly to me, saying he wanted to give me first choice of the uniforms (many of which were very ill-fitting). He took me alone to the storeroom, ahead of the others in my company. There were several corporals to help him. Someone closed the doors, and the sergeant told me to take off my civilian clothes. Since this was not asking me to do anything which contributed to fighting or killing, I obeyed.

Then they took away my clothes and locked them in my suitcase telling a corporal to take it to the post office and mail it to my home.

Now I was without clothes, so they told me to pick out a uniform. I refused and explained why. Then two corporals were told to dress me up in a uniform. It was winter time and the army issued long underwear. I refused to put on the army underwear so they proceeded to put it on me. One man held the underwear open and told me to lift my foot. I refused, so they lifted my foot, and in this way they put all the army clothes on me just as though I were a helpless baby. They didn't button the pants or the coat properly, leaving an extra button at the top and an extra hole at the bottom. I had on the uniform, but I appeared ridiculous because it was not properly adjusted.

After this, they marched me down the street with soldiers lined up on both sides. As I passed, they all made fun of me. It was like a circus to them, and I was like a monkey.

The second basic Biblical reason for nonresistance is love. "Love your enemies," Jesus said in Matt. 5:44. When we love our enemies, is there any one not included in our love?

In one camp where the C.O.'s were segregated in their own camp area with a guard over them, one of the boys received a box of fruit in the mail from his mother.

When he opened the box, the other boys huddled around him expecting to receive a treat from him. The guard was sitting some distance away, but close enough to see and hear what was going on.

The boy who received the box saw an apple near the bottom and digging it out, he told the other boys, "Look, here is the biggest apple in the lot; we'll give this to the corporal (the guard)." One of the boys took it over to him.

The corporal shed tears as he took the apple, saying, "I don't understand you fellows; the way I treated you, and now you give me the largest apple in the box."

I knew that the Holy Spirit filled my heart with love when I received Him at the time of my new birth. "The love of God is shed abroad in our hearts by the Holy Ghost," we are told in Rom. 5:5.

This, of course, does not mean that when we are saved, we will automatically love everyone. I realized very well that although I had the Holy Spirit, I still had much to learn and needed to make an effort myself to live peaceably with my fellowmen. There are two kinds of people in the world—the saved and the unsaved—the loving and the unloving.

It is, of course, a foregone conclusion that if I love my enemy, I will do him no harm. Then how can I kill him even in time of war?

I once heard a preacher say, "The Christian

has no enemies." Wouldn't that have been a smart answer for one of the apostles to give Jesus when He told them to love their enemies! If that preacher meant we must imagine an enemy is a friend and treat him like one, then there is something dishonest about him. If I must make myself believe that an enemy is my friend before I can love him, then there is something wrong with me. This would not be Biblical. The Bible says, "Love your **enemies**." The only person in the world who can do this is a true Christian, one who has God's Holy Spirit in his heart. It's really a miracle of grace to love an enemy.

A missionary lady from Ohio was in a group of people in the Congo being driven on foot to another town by some revolutionaries. The day was hot. She became exhausted, fell, and lay in the grass by the roadside. A large man, an enemy, came along the road and found her lying there. He bent over her with a menacing gesture and snarled, "I will kill you." She replied, "You may kill me if you like, but first I want to tell you that God loves you." That is loving one's enemy.

I can personally testify that God has enabled me on numerous occasions to love my enemies. I can further testify that few things give me more Christian joy than experiencing this love.

Give Not Railing for Railing

5 Additional Reasons

Besides the two basic reasons for Christians to be nonresistant, several others are also given in the Bible.

To take vengeance is wrong. This involves mental or physical harm to another person and, in many cases, involves killing. Rom. 12:19 says, "Dearly beloved, avenge not yourselves, but rather give place unto wrath: for it is written, Vengeance is mine; I will repay, saith the Lord."

Some of us C.O.'s of World War I were abused or tortured in camp. This was part of the game, of course. After the war some people who were never in the draft asked me, "Why didn't you report those officers to the authorities?" This would have undercut my stand against fighting. I answered, "Then where would my nonresistance have been?"

I did report that I was forced to wear the uniform, not because of personal mistreatment, but because I was forced to do wrong in wearing it and wanted to be free of it. In fact, I invited more persecution by reporting that incident. The officers were not penalized for it, but were ordered to give back my civilian clothes.

Taking vengeance as such is not a sin, for God says He will take vengeance. But for me in this dispensation it is a sin, because the Bible forbids it to Christian believers. In the Old Testament we read of occasions when God told His people Israel to destroy their enemies in revenge, but that was not in the Christian era or the New Testament economy. In the Old Testament God gave His people standards for living as a nation in the world. Israel was a theocracy, an earthly nation directly under God. To Christians in this dispensation, God gives a higher call—a call to suffer oppression and let Him be the avenger.

Furthermore, as a follower of Christ, I feel indebted to do what I can to lead others to salvation. This includes those who have wronged me. If I should take vengeance, I would lose the opportunity to win my enemy for Christ. Because of this I lose interest in taking vengeance; by God's grace I will love him instead.

The sacredness of life makes carnal resistance obnoxious to a true Christian. Life comes from God. Life is so valuable that it can be paid for only by another life. Gen. 9:5, 6: "And surely your blood of your lives will I require; at the hand of every beast will I require it, and at the hand of man; at the hand of every man's brother will I require the life of man. Whoso sheddeth man's blood, by man shall his blood be shed: for in the image of God made he man."

By thinking people of all ages, human life was and is considered a sacred trust, more valuable than any other thing. The kidnapper takes advantage of this deep feeling in man and asks whatever he wants. A man will gladly pay any ransom to free his companion or child. Alas, how cheaply the abductor, or the warring nation, or any other killer values life! For a true Christian, injuring, maiming, or killing a fellow human being is unthinkable in any circumstance.

Only God has the right to take human life or to authorize a human to do so. Gen. 9:5, 6 makes this clear. Murder is so serious a crime that God requires the life of a murdered man at the hand of his fellowman. (More will be given on this later.)

Railing is forbidden in I Peter 3:9. "Not

rendering evil for evil, or railing for railing." This means we shall not take part in mouth battles or tongue-lashings. The spirit in a railer is just as evil as the spirit in one who fights with his fists. To take a tongue-lashing from someone without returning the same to him requires grace from God, but you are the victor, not the loser.

One of my friends in India was a pastor of a large congregation. Before he was a Christian, he had been a low-caste Hindu. No one usually thought about this because he was such a kindhearted, devoted Christian. One day he was making pastoral calls to some homes of members. He came to the house where a sister member of the church lived. He called from the yard gate, and this woman, who had some sort of gripe at the pastor, began to rail him shamefully and call him by his low-caste Hindu name. She was very abusive.

He kindly said, "All right, Sister, I will see you some other time," and he went on to another house. In a day or two this sister came to the pastor's house broken and weeping bitterly. She apologized penitently for the way she had treated him. She was the loser, but the Lord be praised that she repented.

If I claim conscientious objection to war but have no hesitancy about answering harsh words with harsh words, I may be making conscience an excuse to cover a deplorable kind of hypocrisy; a desire to be popular by joining the

31

modern anti-war movement; or a fear of going to the battlefield. Or, am I unable to judge properly and so call going to war a big thing, but assaulting a person verbally just a little thing?

The one difference, of course, is that fighting with a gun may kill people physically while a verbal assault will not do this. However, in both cases, my spirit is the same, and both are alike sinful.

I once knew a very good, devoted, older deacon who, with another man, was working as carpenter on the porch of a house by the roadside. A third man whom they both knew well came down the road, stopped his car by the porch, and walked over to the two men. This third man imagined he had just cause for a gripe against the two working men. The two stood up and silently listened to the railing. Finally the railer came to the end of his words. Then the deacon asked him, "Do you have any more to say now?" He answered, "No." The deacon replied, "We don't have anything to say either. You may go now."

Although the unjust accusation could have been justly refuted, how much better it was to listen in silence than give railing for railing!

The general tenor of the New Testament is another very important reason for living the nonresistant life.

To begin with, Bible prophecies concerning the coming, the birth and the childhood of Jesus contain words such as: child, peace, lamb, Saviour, and Jesus. There were no such words as: terrible, judge, tyrant, warrior, or conqueror.

His birth was noted by the peaceful shepherds, and by the friendly wise men from the East. When Herod planned to destroy the child, Joseph and Mary quietly fled with Him to Egypt. When they returned, Jesus grew up as a kindly young man; and when he was grown, He did nothing to stir up any war or just antagonism. Instead, He fed, healed, comforted, forgave, and encouraged the good. He didn't resist the wicked men who crucified Him, but He prayed for their forgiveness. When He appeared in groups, He always spoke peace. But he moved the world!

The New Testament records no wars, although it does predict some for the last days. It is full of teachings on peace and nonresistance. It glorifies martyrs and those martyred for the sake of the Gospel, and in its prophecies pronounces doom on those who kill and destroy. The epistles are geared toward gathering together, unifying and comforting God's people. The serious reader of the New Testament is impelled to live peaceably with all men.

The preaching or proclaiming the good news of salvation as taught in the New Testament is one of the strongest arguments against carnal resistance. It is the very opposite. The primary work prescribed for God's people in the New

Testament is stated in Matt. 28:19, 20, "Go ye therefore, and teach all nations, baptizing them in the name of the Father, and of the Son, and of the Holy Ghost: Teaching them to observe all things whatsoever I have commanded you."

It would be a gross contradiction for me to be a preacher of the Gospel and also take part in war. What a spectacle I would be—preaching the Gospel of life with a Bible in one hand and a gun in the other. Can I both kill and bring life?

I have a very good friend and relative who, as an officer in the army, took his Bible wherever he went and conducted Sunday schools and Bible studies. He later saw this inconsistency and regretted the army part of his career.

In bygone years, and perhaps even now, some pastors professing to preach the Gospel also urged their young men to join the armed services. This presents a ridiculous contradiction, for the total thrust of the Gospel is life-giving and peace, healing and love, while war is the very opposite.

This reminds me of one Hindu deity who found himself in the predicament of having to go into battle when his own relatives were on the opposing side. He went to a higher deity and opened his problem for counsel. He told the higher deity that it was his duty to fight for his country, but since it is wrong to kill one's own kin, he was caught in a bind. The higher deity told him that it would be no difficult problem.

His advice was in effect, "Just take your sword and turn your face toward the enemy lines. Then close your eyes and move forward, swinging your sword. If you don't see your kin and so kill them, it will not be your fault."

That is pagan philosophy. The true Christian does not get into such a bind because God's Word for him is clear and consistent.

In the Old Testament dispensation, God's people Israel were not commissioned to preach the Gospel. They were God's earthly kingdom. He wanted them to be an ideal earthly nation.

In the New Dispensation the people of God, the church, are God's heavenly people on earth, and their work is to preach the Gospel—to make disciples.

Israel used military power under God. The church makes disciples by the power of love, through the Holy Spirit and the Word of God.

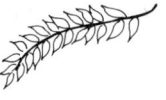

Go with Him Two Miles

6 Related Involvements

There are some other aspects of nonresistance which do not deal directly with war or retaliation, but which also need to be considered.

Being willing to go the second mile is one facet of nonresistant living. In Matt. 5:41 Jesus said, "And whosoever shall compel thee to go a mile, go with him twain."

Another name for such compelling is "forced labor," or making one work without pay. In some eastern countries we find the practice of wealthy people and officials requiring services from poorer people without paying for the work. We do not have this practice in a literal sense in America, but we have many abuses that involve the same principle. For instance, one time I made a purchase and I was cheated. I didn't get my money's worth. Then I said, "I'm not going back to that place any more." So I went out of my way and farther from home to get the article when I needed another one. The Spirit convicted me and I repented. After that I went back to the first place and bought there again. I wasn't cheated that time although I had given the dealer an opportunity. Belatedly, I went the second mile.

When I was in India, this incident occurred in the villages. An Indian official—a circuit judge—traveled over his district, holding court in a number of villages. He had boxes and bags with his food, clothes, bedding, books and whatever else he needed on such tours. Since he traveled on foot, he couldn't carry all his luggage. He remained one or more days in a village, before moving on to the next village. When he was ready to move on, he got some peasants and farmers to carry his luggage for him, then dismissed them without pay. This was the general understanding so no one objected too much. Each time he moved he used men from the village he was leaving.

Once he came to a village where some Christian people lived. When, after a couple of

37

days, he wanted to move to the next village, he saw some healthy looking boys and asked them to carry his baggage. He didn't realize they were Christians, but I suppose he would have asked them even if he had known it. They obliged him and took his luggage to the next village. When they arrived, he told them they can go back home. However, the boys refused, and said, "We'll take your things to the next village when you are ready to go." He objected, saying, "I'll get men from here to carry my things tomorrow," but the boys insisted they wanted to stay.

The judge was very much perplexed and said, "Who are you? What kind of people are you? I never before met people who wanted to do more than I asked of them." The boys told him they were Christians and that Jesus told them to do it that way. The one boy had a Testament in his shirt pocket so he opened it to Matt. 5:41 and showed it to the judge. He still could not understand how they could do this. As a non-Christian, he couldn't understand Christian ways.

This Scripture teaches that if anyone requires something from us unjustly, we are to do even more for him than he asked of us. I have gone the second mile often enough that I know by experience it is good for the soul. We are happier when it is done, and God our Father is glorified. No doubt some will say, "But how can we do this and survive?" My only answer is that the

Lord has promised He will not allow us to be tried more severely than we are able to bear. The only right course for me is to obey God's Word and trust Him for my future.

To sue at the law is forbidden in I Cor. 6:7 where it says, "Now therefore there is utterly a fault among you, because ye go to law one with another. Why do ye not rather take wrong? why do ye not rather suffer yourselves to be defrauded?"

I have a good friend who is a building contractor, an honest builder of good houses. One time he built a house for a man who asked the privilege of moving into the house before he had paid quite all that he had agreed to pay before taking possession. My friend, being an honest man himself, took the man's word that he would pay the five hundred dollars later. After some time the contractor went for the money. This man's reply was, "Yes, I know I owe you five hundred dollars, but you get it from me! I will pay if you take it to court, but not otherwise." The man may have known that my friend would not go to court to collect a bill. He didn't pay so my friend wrote it off as a bad debt. How much happier he was by not going to court than if he had violated God's Word to collect the money!

Going to law does not necessarily result in taking life unless it involves capital punishment. However, it is a form of carnal resistance that the Bible forbids to Christians. This is very hard for some people to see, but the Lord says it is better to allow ourselves to be cheated. Suing at the law is wrong because it is using force to exact from my neighbor what he is unwilling to give me.

If I take someone before the judge, the result will usually be the same regardless of whether I win the case or lose it. I will likely have made an enemy of that person, at least not a friend. The question should be, "Have I helped that person be more open to receiving the Gospel or have I just made an enemy a worse enemy?" It will likely be more difficult for me to win that man to Christ. If I sue a Christian brother, as the text really implies, would I encourage or discourage him? If he needs some correction as a brother, I should take him before the church, and not before sinners.

To me, an open door to talk to my enemy about salvation would be much more valuable than the dollars or goods I might exact from him by force of the law.

A ready and willing spirit of forgiveness is always found in the person with a truly nonresistant mind.

An Old Order Amish minister, some years ago, went to church one night with horse and buggy. He tied his horse to the hitching rail outside the church and went inside to worship. During the service some mischievous young boys were in the church yard "horsing around." Two of these boys gathered rocks and piled them in the back part of the minister's buggy, filling it up and weighting it down.

When church was over, the minister untied his horse and started down the road toward home. After he had gone a short distance, he noticed there was unusual weight to his buggy. Stopping the horse, he silently unloaded the rocks and left them at the roadside. He soon forgot about the rock incident, but twenty years later one of these "boys" came to the minister and made apology for loading the stones into his buggy saying, "My conscience kept troubling me all the time."

The minister, now an old man, simply replied, "What a pity you carried those 'rocks' in your mind all these twenty years, when I threw them out of the buggy that same night!"

It's hard to pick a quarrel with someone who forgives you immediately when you wrong him. In the model prayer Jesus gave in Matt. 6, He tells us to pray, "Forgive us our debts, as we forgive our debtors." According to this, we need expect no forgiveness from God if we can't forgive those who work against us.

The spirit of forgiveness is an essential element in the nonresistant life. For both mental and spiritual health's sake I must deal with opposition that comes to me. If someone wrongs me and I only suppress my feeling or become a silent martyr but do nothing about it, later on there may be some serious negative reaction. A non-Christian psychiatrist says that for the sake of mental health you must fight back. This may, of course, prevent the negative reaction that results from silently suppressing one's hurt feelings, but it will start a chain of other bad effects. The way for the natural man may be to fight back, but that isn't the best answer. A Christian has the perfect way to deal with such a situation. Through the Spirit of Christ in him, he handles the case with love and forgiveness. This is the way to remove the offense for good.

A small scale illustration of this came into my experience. I was unjustly accused by a co-worker of telling an untruth. I can testify for the glory of God that I forgave him sincerely even before he apologized. By God's help I put his offense out of the way, and I feel free; I love my co-worker. I believe I am wholly honest in saying this.

Although Stephen the deacon may never have studied psychology, he practiced the highest quality of mental health therapy when he prayed to God, "Lord, lay not this sin to their charge." These were his last words as he was being stoned to death by his enemies. This is marvelous, sterling, and noble! He could do this because he had Christ in his heart. What a victorious way to die!

The sergeant in Camp Greenleaf one day gave

me an order I could not obey conscientiously. When I refused, he told me to follow him. He took me to the bath house and locked all the doors, so no one but he and I were in the building. Then he asked me a question I couldn't conscientiously answer the way he wanted me to answer. When I answered, he hit me in the face with his right hand and with his left hand held me by the hair so I wouldn't fall down. He asked another question, and that time hit me with his fist. He repeated this several times. Once, I remember, he knocked my head against the wall. By the time he stopped hitting me, I felt dizzy, my lips were cut, and my nose was bleeding. Later I had two black eyes.

Recently a young man asked me, "You surely felt anger or resentment against that sergeant, didn't you?" After thinking a bit to recall how I felt at the time, I replied, "I'm sure I felt no anger or resentment against him." This young man said he didn't believe me. Just as I forgave that sergeant the day he hit me, I now forgave this young man for not believing me when I told the truth!

No one else ever loved people like Jesus Christ loved. No one ever did as much for people. No other one was ever so cruelly treated and so falsely accused. No one else could have so well defended Himself against his enemies. But they nailed Him to the cross to destroy Him. While He was being nailed to the cross, He prayed,

"Father, forgive them; for they know not what they do." In this cruel ordeal Jesus was the supreme example of nonresistance. At the moment when the blow was hardest, He forgave them for it all. He didn't wait for them to make apology. He forgave; we must, too.

To suffer loss is often the lot of a nonresistant Christian. Matt. 5:40 says that if someone sues me at the law and takes away my coat, I am to give him my cloak also. This doesn't mean that I become irritated because my coat was taken away, then hand him the overcoat also and say, "There take that, too." It means that I should humbly and sincerely offer the overcoat also if I see he could use it. This is an illustration of the spirit I should have whenever I am forced to lose something of mine. I don't think it means that I should start indiscriminately giving things to any kind of man who asks in any kind of situation. It does mean that I must be willing to suffer loss rather than fight back or appeal to the court for redress.

To agree with my adversary is another part of nonresistance. Matt. 5:25, 26 says, "Agree with thine adversary quickly, whiles thou art in the way with him; lest at any time the adversary deliver thee to the judge, and the judge deliver thee to the officer, and thou be cast into prison. Verily I say unto thee, thou shalt by no means come out thence, till thou hast paid the uttermost farthing."

This teaching obviously does not refer to times when I would be forbidden to preach or exercise my duty toward God. How could I agree with such an adversary? It is referring to a time when an adversary has a claim against me such as demanding payment. It is not stated whether the claim is just or unjust. Since a Christian should never neglect paying his just dues, it appears that the claim of the adversary here is unjust.

Some time ago an accident between a farm tractor and a school bus from a Mennonite Christian School in Ohio caused some damage to the tractor and injury to the tractor driver. All witnesses, including the drivers of both vehicles, agreed that the tractor driver was at fault. Later someone who was not involved encouraged the farmer to change his mind and claim payment for damages. It was clearly an unjust claim.

The farmer demanded thirty-five hundred dollars from the church. The church leaders tried to come to a better agreement with him but failed, so the demand was fully met by the church rather than go to court. Public sentiment in the community favored the church, so a good testimony was left. I witnessed this incident as I was a teacher in the school.

The main point in this Matt. 5 teaching is that I should agree with the adversary as soon as possible, thus keeping out of court and out of jail. To agree with the adversary "whiles thou art in the way," means to agree while you can still talk with him, before the case goes to court.

There are different ways to agree with an adversary. Once in an automobile collision, one person involved was a good deacon in the church. Obviously the other man was at fault, but it began to appear that he would sue for payment of damages so the deacon quickly said, "I think it would be best for each of us to fix his own car." The adversary agreed and seemed to be relieved. With this peaceable settlement, there was no need for any court or judge. The deacon who could justly have claimed damages from the other man, paid for his own car repair. He suffered some financial loss, but he gained much more. The other man was friendly after that. By avoiding court, he also strengthened the witness of the church and reflected the spirit of Christ.

"Thou shalt not kill," is one of the ten commandments. In Numbers 35:16-28 we get the concept that when one purposely kills another human being out of enmity or rage, he commits murder.

This commandment is quoted by Jesus in Matt. 19:18, "Thou shalt do no murder." Not all killing of humans is murder. The Israelites and the Patriarchs before them were told to punish the murderer by killing him. They weren't told to murder the murderer. The Bible clearly makes a difference in killing. Sometimes it is murder, and sometimes it is not murder.

For the Christian, it is true, all killing—from abortion, to murdering an adult or capital punishment—is sin. For a civil officer, some killing is illegal, and some is legal. According to Christ's teaching, it is just as wrong for New Testament believers to kill an enemy soldier in battle as to murder a civilian. Both the Old Testament and our modern civil laws make a difference in this. It is noteworthy in this respect that murder is considered wrong in all countries of the world. This concept began with the case of Cain and Abel when God gave the command of capital punishment for murder in Gen. 9:5, 6.

Another phase of murder which is often ignored is taught in I John 3:15, "Whosoever hateth his brother is a murderer: and ye know that no murderer hath eternal life abiding in him." The matter of sinful killing is more than only the physical act.

When I hate someone, I am just as guilty as if I had killed him, even though he still lives. I tend to minimize the sinfulness of hating when I am not killing anyone, but I am still guilty as a murderer. I need to be careful lest while I claim conscientious objections to war, I fall into the error of hating those who oppose me in my stand.

No true conscientious objector to war will ever call a police officer a "pig." Neither will he judge a government official as immoral because he is an official of a government waging war. When I have a heart filled with love, I do not judge others in ways like these.

A C.O. friend of mine in the first World War had his bunk next to the wall in a wooden barracks building. This wall was only a board partition between his room and the officers' office room, and one day he heard the officers discussing the conscientious objectors. One of them said, "The trouble is that we can't make them angry or talk back to us. If we could make them talk back, we could court martial them." This speaks eloquently about our attitudes toward government officials.

The matter of capital punishment is completely outside the realm of Christian faith and practice. As has been stated, capital punishment for murder was instituted by God, and continues to be a part of civil rulers' responsibility. The church is a completely different entity operating in a different realm and on a different basis.

That nations in Old Testament times often practiced the shedding of man's blood by man under the authority of God is recorded in many passages. Also there were numerous instances in which God commanded Israel to destroy certain people in war. There are other cases also where God either commanded or allowed certain nations to fall on other nations to punish them.

I understand from the Bible that taking human life is so serious that only God has the right to do it or to delegate certain people to do it. Capital punishment must be counted in this category.

Some of the fightings and oppressions of Old Testament times even under God's command sound gruesome to some of us Christians today, but they are historical facts, and we cannot question God.

It is always painful for a Christian to see anyone killed—not from the sentimental point of view only, but because of the new nature given to him when the Holy Spirit fills his heart with love for all men. When a Christian sees a murderer, his first impulse is to give him the Gospel of forgiveness and peace with God—to see him saved rather than executed in his sinful condition! What a testimony it would be for Christ and His church if we Christians would make it our regular practice to visit criminals in prison, striving to lead them to salvation before they are executed!

I have known some cases where prisoners were visited by Christian workers and were converted. This should be known as our general practice! Let us fulfill our role as a church; then we will be less concerned about the civil officer's method of carrying out his role.

It is, however, highly inconsistent for Christians to be critical of civil officers for executing a murderer. For God commanded capital punishment after the flood (Gen. 9:6), gave it as a part of the Law to the nation of Israel (Ex. 21:12), and arranged (ordained) the civil power as an avenger to bear the sword upon the evildoer (Rom. 13:1-4). It is a necessity for a sinful society, that violence may be curbed.

But the Christian avenges not and overcomes evil with good. This does not mean that God has two ethical standards for man to live by or to be judged by. Rather, man chooses—either the kingdom of this world or the church of Jesus Christ. It is impossible to ulitmately control the kingdom of this world by the law of love and forgiveness. Yet, for the Christian not to love and forgive is sin. Thus the Christian leaves the punishment of the evildoer, including capital punishment, to the rulers in the kingdoms of this world, and is not critical of them for doing it.

I will never agree to serve as a juror, especially in cases involving capital punishment.

We witness to rulers and government officers as well as to anyone else. All men, including officials, need the same Gospel, for all are lost without Christ.

I read in Matt. 14:1-12 that John the Baptist told Herod, who had taken his brother Philip's wife, "It is not lawful for thee to have her." This finally resulted in John the Baptist's losing his life. It does seem that when a man of God speaks to someone, even to a governor or some other high official, his word counts for something. It seems to me in this account John the

Baptist did not defame or belittle Herod, but tried to help him personally to live right morally. I believe John the Baptist spoke to Herod quietly without a demonstration or drawing public attention to him.

From studying the New Testament Scriptures we conclude that when Christians try to shape or reshape the state's policies and activities, they act outside of their sphere. This is especially true when they take part in protest demonstrations, lobbying, boycotts, or other unchristian activities. When necessity arises they can make requests or petitions by legitimate means for consideration in certain cases such as exemption from military service, jury service or any laws or measures which would cause them to violate their Christian conscience.

It is not consistent with true evangelical faith to expect officers to conduct the affairs of state on the basis of Christian principles at all times. We like to see this done where possible, but we cannot demand it. It is no more proper to expect the state to control a dangerous criminal by love and gentleness than to expect the church to threaten its members with a jail sentence if they do not take part in communion.

According to some people today, Jesus would have had sufficient reasons to order Caesar to cease oppression of the Jews and to change his tactics and foreign policies. But He didn't.

The most effective way for Christian citizens

to influence our government, or the state in any country, is to live in a way that commands the respect of neighbors and state officials. In our country we do not lose respect of officials by refusing to take up arms for the state when they know we have genuine Christian convictions against it, and live consistently in all phases of life.

A certain corporal in Camp Greenleaf was very harsh, opposing me in various ways. When I was discharged after the war, I changed trains at the P.R.R. station in Pittsburgh. The station was jammed with people. As I was going from one train to the other one, a young man came out of the crowd and extended his hand for a handshake. He asked me whether I recognized him and was surprised that I didn't. Then he said, "I was Corporal _____ in Camp Greenleaf, and I was discharged a few weeks ago. When I found out you were coming through Pittsburgh tonight on your way home, I came here to apologize for the way I treated you in camp." I assured him that I had no ill feelings toward him.

We are told to overcome evil with good, Rom. 12:21. God doesn't ask me to be a coward; I am to be an overcomer. The Holy Spirit does not make a Christian passive, permissive, weakly, easygoing, spineless, chickenhearted, and wishy-washy. God uses strong characters and personalities. We are told to overcome our enemies—not by shooting them, but by doing them good.

Once I heard of a farmer who bought a farm in a community where he was not acquainted. After he bought it, he chanced to talk with some neighbors who informed him that his next-farm neighbor would be very difficult. He was already an enemy. They had heard this difficult neighbor already talking against the new neighbor who bought the farm. The new neighbor replied that he was not much worried. "I'll kill him," he said. The neighbors were afraid to ask what he meant. The difficult neighbor, too, heard in a roundabout way what the new neighbor had said. Some time later the difficult neighbor's barn was struck by lightning and started to burn. Promptly the new neighbor went over, braving the storm, and helped save as much cattle and goods as possible. He offered the use of his own barn to shelter his neighbor's cattle temporarily. Soon after that tragedy, another misfortune hit the old neighbor and again the new neighbor went to his aid. After this type of thing occurred several times, the two men became fast friends. Although other neighbors could never get along with him, the new neighbor "killed" his enemy by changing him into a friend.

I heard also of a Christian man who bought property in a city. The day after he moved, his next-door neighbor came over. "Did you know," he asked, "that the hedge between our lots is eight inches on my side? This gives you eight inches of my land." The new neighbor replied, "Why no, I didn't know that! Let's go out right now and see where the correct line is. I'll move the hedge back."

The neighbor was completely disarmed. "If you're going to be that kind to me, we'll just leave the hedge where it is," he said.

Although some enemies cannot be overcome with good, this method is more effective than fighting back. We as Christians must follow this course for conscience sake. It is more than just the best way to keep a healthy conscience, it is the way to be a true witness of the Gospel.

"Whosoever shall say, Thou fool shall be in danger of hell fire" (Matt. 5:22). One form of carnal resistance is to curse or to blaspheme an enemy—real or imagined. No true Christian will curse anyone, because he loves his enemy and desires to see him saved.

To call someone a fool is to put him down as low as possible. Basically, the word "fool" means one who knows nothing. This puts a man even lower than an animal. The real meaning of the word "fool" is not simply the opposite of "wise," even though it is often used that way. Someone might say about another—"He was a fool for buying that property"—meaning he didn't use good judgment. In such a case, it is not so severe. A similar statement would be, "I made a fool of myself when I meddled."

If I, in anger, call a man a fool, I am not only

utterly despising him, I am also reflecting on God who made the man.

It is no wonder then that one who says, "You fool," is in danger of hell fire. By his attitude he is committing murder in his heart. No Christian will use such belittling and degrading invectives on others.

"Resist not evil," is part of Matt. 5:39. In verses 38 and 39 we have these words, "Ye have heard that it hath been said, An eye for an eye, and a tooth for a tooth: But I say unto you, That ye resist not evil; but whosoever shall smite thee on thy right cheek, turn to him the other also."

From the 39th verse we take the name "nonresistance" for this New Testament doctrine. This means that if someone does me wrong, I am not to resist him (by carnal means). That takes more strength than to hit back.

This passage also says that if someone hits me on the right cheek, I am to turn to him the other also. It doesn't say that I am to ask someone to hit me again, but it means that I give him an opportunity. My enemy might be someone who forbids me to talk to people about Christ as the way of salvation. He might even hit me in the face. If I continue talking to people about Christ, I would then be doing what would seem to me a practical way to turn the other cheek.

In Camp Greenleaf one evening I received an order to report for KP duty the next morning at five o'clock. Because this would be contributing to the military, I felt it was wrong for me to work even in the kitchen. The next morning I presented myself at the mess hall. The mess sergeant was there too, earlier than usual, possibly anticipating that I would refuse to work. I explained to him why I couldn't do this work. He questioned me and scolded for a while, then told me to go back to my tent and rot. Later I got an order to work the next day, but this time he told me to stand at attention in the mess hall. So I stood at attention in the mess hall all that day with time off only to eat. All the soldiers came there to eat; and while they were eating, some laughed; some scowled; some cursed; some asked me, in mockery, to pray. I kept on standing at attention, but this becomes difficult when one must stand more than a few minutes.

I suppose the sergeant thought that I would be broken down, so he put me on the slate again the third morning. I refused again, so he made me stand at attention again. While I didn't think of it then, this was probably turning the other cheek, for I let him make me stand at attention the second time.

You might ask, "How long can I suffer such treatment and keep my self-respect or even survive physically?" Where do you think God is when you get your tooth or eye knocked out or get your face slapped? Don't think for a moment that our heavenly Father will tell us to do such a dangerous thing and then forsake us.

Even though God might even let someone take advantage of me for a while, would I be justified in defending myself? As a Christian I might even lose all my possessions or even my life. Basically, that is not the issue. The issue is my attitude. Job lost all but his life, and that hung only on a thread. What was Job's attitude? "The Lord gave, and the Lord hath taken away; blessed be the name of the Lord." I pray that I may maintain such an attitude.

Nowhere in the New Testament does God promise that no trouble will come to us if we obey. My orders from heaven are to turn the other cheek. It might even be good for me spiritually if my enemy would hit me on the other cheek over and over again. What strength of personality that would develop!

Probably you know that most dogs bite only out of fear. People are just like dogs in this respect. When I strike back, I prove I am afraid, and I have really lost the battle. I am told that when two Chinese fight, they will refrain from hitting each other as long as they can, for the first one to hit the other is considered to have lost the fight. This illustration has one weak point because for Christians a mouth battle is as sinful as a fist battle.

"**Pray for them which despitefully use you,** and persecute you" (Matt. 5:44), is another essential element in living nonresistantly. Praying for one who opposes you is no doubt the truest expression of returning good for evil.

Returning good for evil by smiling, saying something kind, showing courtesy, giving a gift or helping one in difficulty are all commendable ways to carry out this precept. However, any of these could possibly be done with comparative ease or they could be done insincerely in order to make a show or to pretend. But secretly praying for one's enemy would hardly be insincere. Praying for the good of my enemy is a positive way to practice nonresistance. It is doing something good, not only refraining from resistance by carnal means.

In Camp Greenleaf in 1918, I was one of nineteen conscientious objectors segregated in one corner of the camp. We were treated as prisoners with a guard over us. One young man of our group was John Bergen, from Oklahoma, who was never fortunate enough to go to school or learn to read and write, but was nevertheless wise in spiritual matters. He suffered more than any of the rest of us for his stand against fighting or killing. One rainy day Sergeant M_____ hit him in the head with his fist and knocked him down in the mud. Then the sergeant kicked him in the chest several times, broke some ribs, and split his breast bone. He dragged him to the bath house and put him under the cold shower to wash the mud off his clothes, then put him on his cot in the tent. But the boy received no medical help.

At another time the same sergeant hit him in the face and broke his nose. It healed, but was crooked.

Still another time he hit him in the face and knocked his head against a 2 x 4 stud of the wall, breaking his jawbone. This time the sergeant saw that he was taken to the hospital. There a doctor set his jawbone and tied his upper and lower teeth together with gold wire. His teeth were wired that way for six weeks before he was discharged from the hospital. The day after he came back to us he was forced to stand at attention in the hot sun all day. Before it ended he stood at attention for two or three days, with time off just to eat and sleep.

A few days later the sergeant put a rope around John's neck and over a limb of a pine tree. Then he pulled steadily on the rope to raise his feet off the ground, but was careful not to break his neck. Soon John became unconscious. Then he was let down and laid face down on the ground. The sergeant used a cattle whip on his back until he came to consciousness again. In addition, there were many minor ways in which he was tortured.

It was our custom to hold regular prayer meetings in one of our tents. I especially remember John's audible prayer at one meeting—one of the most moving prayers I ever heard. With his teeth still wired together, he spent most of his turn praying for Sergeant M____. He prayed, and wept, that God would bless him and that he would some day be saved.

In such a situation this kind of praying could have been done only by one who knew Christ in reality. Since the sergeant, of course, was never present at any of our prayer meetings, we know John prayed sincerely, not just to impress the sergeant.

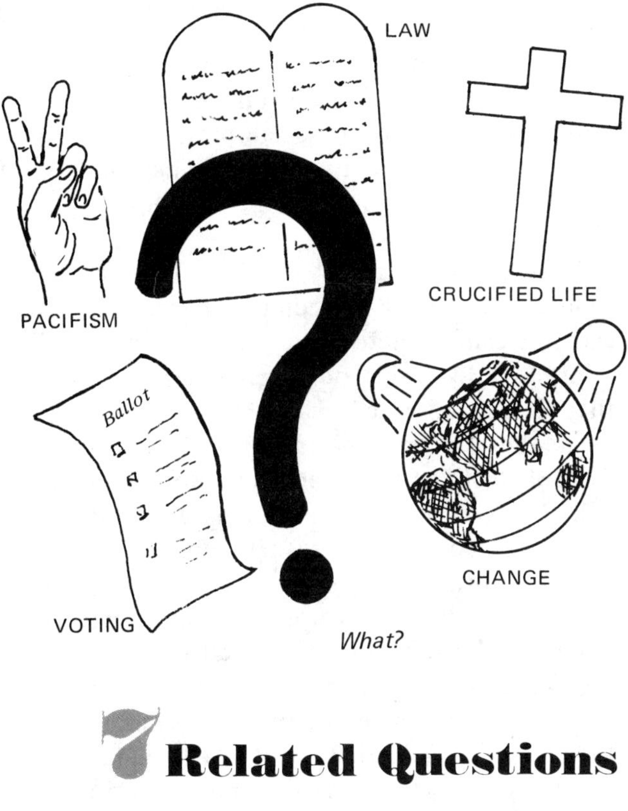

PACIFISM · LAW · CRUCIFIED LIFE · VOTING · CHANGE · *What?*

7 Related Questions

Many questions are asked regarding this doctrine of nonresistance. Since questions help to clear our minds of doubts, a few such questions will be considered in this chapter.

Was Jesus a pacifist?

Many people's interpretation of New Testament teaching on peace has been markedly influenced by the current popular mood of

61

pacifism and anti-war sentiment as well as the rioting and demonstrations we have witnessed.

A person is unstable when he is influenced by popular sentiment or social pressure. As for Bible interpretation, it is safest to interpret the Bible by the Bible through the Holy Spirit. This gives poise.

First, let us consider what Jesus Himself said, "Think not that I am come to send peace on earth: I came not to send peace, but a sword" (Matt. 10:34). This obviously does not mean that Jesus promoted wars. It does, however, mean that He promotes a different kind of life from that of the world and, therefore, conflicts will come, even between parents and children. The Christian life is so far superior to life without Christ that disharmony is unavoidable. It seems to me that Christ is really saying He would not accommodate Himself to those who oppose Him, nor would He compromise for the sake of peace. On the other hand, some people today are so pacifistic they would go a long way to be at peace with those who oppose Christ.

It is true, we Christians are to live peaceably with all men as far as possible on our part, but when our being at peace with others causes us to lose our peace with God, then we must keep our peace with God, regardless of our opponents.

Jesus was not a pacifist. He did not advocate peace at any cost. Because He was called the Prince of Peace is no reason to think that He came to establish peace between God and God's enemies unless God's enemies would yield to God which, of course, is precisely why He did come into the world. Through Christ we are reconciled to God, so in this sense He is the Prince of Peace.

Does the New Testament give instructions or standards for rulers of the state?

I do not find any New Testament teaching as the standard of conduct for earthly rulers. The salvation of the lost and establishing of the church are the primary concerns of the Gospels and Acts. A notable example of this is the high-priestly prayer of Jesus in John 17. Basic principles and applications for Christian living make up practically all the rest of the New Testament. These include the various doctrines and disciplines, ordinances for the church, and spiritual truths for the nurture of the saints.

Romans 13 is one passage that contains some enlightenment concerning the state. This passage is obviously not meant as a directive for worldly governments, but is given to point out part of the Christian's duty toward the state. It states that the powers that be are ordained of God. Also, that earthly rulers are not meant to be a terror to good works but to the evil. The purposeful bearing of the sword by law officers is also mentioned.

The fact that God is still concerned for earthly government is revealed when it says that the powers are ordained of God. He also tells us as Christians to be subject to these powers, not only for fear, but for conscience sake.

To me it is highly significant that so little is mentioned in the New Testament about earthly rulers and their duties. To put it in a single statement, the subject of the New Testament is God's concern for the church.

The form and substance of Old Testament doctrine are different from those of the New Testament. Instructions for civil rulership and standards for the theocracy of Israel occupy a good share of the Old Testament.

We have no suggestion anywhere in the Bible that God's will for worldly rulers today is different from what it was for Old Testament governments. That the same standards are carried forward to New Testament times is at least assumed when the New Testament says, "He beareth not the sword in vain: for he is the minister of God" (Rom. 13:4).

Should a Christian vote for public officials?

To this question not everyone has yet found an answer. Those who think they have found the answer do not agree among themselves. Some vote, some do not. Some vote on certain issues, or vote for the more desirable candidate when they think the other candidate is very far from desirable.

Several times officers said to me when I was a conscientious objector in camp, "You voted for the President, you should now support him by fighting." I was glad I could say that I never voted in my life.

Of course, the question whether it is right or wrong to vote comes up in those who recognize the church and the state as two distinct entities or those who are conscientious objectors to war.

To me it seems highly inconsistent to help elect the command-in-chief of the army and navy, when I refuse to take part in the military. Some may say I am really voting for the president of our country and not for a military officer. This satisfies some people's conscience, but the fact still remains that I am part of the church, and he is the head of the state.

This does not mean that I should remain entirely passive and unconcerned as to who would become our president. As a Christian, I am concerned for the good of the people and for the privilege to preach the Gospel and to live by its precepts, so naturally I am deeply concerned that the right person be elected.

Some others may be interested in personal gain or advantage and so work hard to help elect the one they think will promote their causes. Some people become so wrought up over an election they act irrationally. Some fanatics even attempt to assassinate the candidate they do not want. All this human fervor usually ends with a punctured balloon or perhaps an assassin in prison and a shocking funeral.

As a Christian, I am constrained to give myself to prayer that God will so direct in the election that His chosen man be elected to that important office. If I vote, I count for one in millions. If I pray for God's direction, I may influence thousands of voters. God knows better than I who is the right man for the place. God will do what I cannot do. Some may call this mysticism. I call it faith.

Let us all pray at each election time that God's chosen man might be elected. This is one of the most important ways in which we can be the salt of the earth. If we think Christian people should be a stronger influence in choosing our rulers, this is the most effective way to do it.

Also, I do not mean to say that if I vote for the president, I am thereby obliged to obey him in everything, but it would appear more consistent if I would do so.

I believe that to be consistent with the concept of a separate church and state, I should not vote. I acknowledge that, in a measure, I am a citizen of my country, but my first citizenship is in the heavenly kingdom. When I pray for our government, I am carrying out one of the very important precepts of the kingdom of God, for this is what God tells the Christian to do.

Does God change?

The same principles that God gave for Old Testament saints were preserved for New Testament saints. In giving us the New Testament standards, Jesus never condemns the standards of the Old Testament, but lifts them to the highest plane. This is obvious in Matt. 5. These are now the standards for His called-out people to whom He gives the power to keep them.

The Old Testament saints were involved in a form of government called a theocracy—an earthly nation ruled directly by God. New Testament saints are not an earthly theocracy, but a church, which is a living organism.

All this does not indicate that God has a double standard for human living. It rather indicates God's consistently unified economy for a world with two kinds of people. He is both just and merciful. He would have all men saved by His mercy, but not all men accept His salvation.

Neither does all this say that God changes. Rather, that God doesn't change is proven by the structure of His economy. If God would change, then He would cease to be God. He is absolute. He does not work by trial and error. He knows the end from the beginning. God changes only His ways of dealing with men; His ideals, standards, and principles never change.

In some matters God bears with the weakness of man for a time as in the case of divorce being permitted or commanded for Israel in Old Testament times. He told Moses to write them a bill of divorcement, but said, "From the beginning it was not so" (Matt. 19:8). This allowance was made because of the hardness of hearts in Israel.

Some students have held that God's approval of war and the taking of human life in Old Testament times was given on the same basis as the matter of divorce. However, it should be observed that the two matters are different. God's command in Gen. 9:6 could not fit into such a category at all—"Whoso sheddeth man's blood, by man shall his blood be shed."

Oh how I appreciate the God who never changes! This is a source of real security. I can trust to obey Him and trust Him for my safekeeping in a hostile world. To be identified with the unchanging God of the universe gives me confidence, poise, assurance, and a great hope through Jesus Christ.

What is the real spiritual significance of the doctrine of nonresistance?

I believe every teaching, concept, or ordinance given to us by God carries a definite meaning or significance. God doesn't give us any rules to keep only for the sake of the rules. Jesus answered the Pharisees by saying that the Sabbath was made for man and not man for the Sabbath. It signified the coming of Christ in whom we have our rest. The Sabbath really was made for man. In the same way every doctrine or rule of the Bible given by God is for our spiritual good.

It seems to me that the teaching on nonresistance is even broader and more inclusive in its meaning for us than many of the other New Testament disciplines. I think, because of this, some Christians tend to overemphasize the importance of it to the extent they seem to feel that either embracing this doctrine or being a strong pacifist will somehow make one a child of God. I would admit that acceptance of this doctrine seems to involve some of the principles of salvation, but we must also be aware that some who do not know Christ or even profess faith in Him do profess to be strong pacifists. These persons often seem sincere, but when it comes to a real test, their genuineness fades out.

It gives me a great deal of spiritual satisfaction that when I practice this teaching I am really living out a great concept involved in God's plan of salvation. When I let an enemy hit me without retaliation, absorb his blow and still love him, I show by living example just how God forgives and saves. This is a profound and glorious experience for which I praise God!

The attitude of a nonresistant person also shows strength of character. As I stated earlier, the person who can take a blow without retaliating is strong, while striking back or even killing the opponent is only an illustration of man's weakness. The honeybee that stings an enemy will likely lose its stinger and die. This is not strength. It is weakness. It is sad to think of how many honeybees have died uselessly while the people they stung are living on. Yet some people would idealize such an act and call it bravery when a man is willing to give his life to get rid of an enemy. If the bee could have reasoned a bit and refrained from stinging, thus saving its own life and saving the man from discomfort, it would have been a "super bee," and the world would have had more honey through it.

A man proves he has very little trust in God's keeping power when he resorts to violence to save himself. It is true that when we trust God for food, we must perhaps plant potatoes, weed them, hoe them, dig them, and cook them before we can benefit from them. So working goes with faith in God. But there is a great difference between raising potatoes and killing a man in self-defense. Killing is not a work of faith, but a violation of God's commands; for God told us not to kill, but to preach the Gospel.

Living the nonresistant life toward our fellowman is one of the most effective ways to show our love to him. Of course, it is genuine nonresistance when it is motivated by love—the brand of nonresistance that has real meaning. There could be a kind of nonresistance which springs from fear or cowardice, but that will not hold in the final test. Even a coward will ultimately strike back when he can no longer outrun his enemy.

Selfishness and true nonresistance are not compatible. In fact, they cannot live together in the same heart. Nothing in a man is more noble than willingness to lay down his life for the sake of another. By the same token, nothing is more ignoble than killing a fellowman out of selfishness.

To die for the sake of another is the real spirit of Christ. Christ came to earth to give Himself for lost man. What a marvelous opportunity God gives to me as a Christian—to advertise the great work of Christ my Lord by living nonresistantly!

There are, of course, various ways to testify of Christ's living in me, but it is doubtful that one can find a more effective way than bearing and absorbing an enemy's blow without retaliation, because we love him. Some people say that it is things we do such as speaking in tongues, that prove our genuineness as children of God. Speaking in tongues can be counterfeited by the devil, but I never heard of a counterfeit giving of one's life for an enemy.

When I was a conscientious objector in the army camp, soldier boys who didn't understand me called me the "preacher," in derision. I was not an ordained man then, but it is interesting that at least they associated my behavior with Christianity.

On one occasion a uniformed soldier, a corporal, apologized to me for having helped to put the army uniform on me against my will. Something made him repent in his heart.

My prayer is that what I have written might help to give some young people—or older—the satisfaction and fulness of joy I have found in obeying Christ's teaching of nonresistance.

Christian Light Publications, Inc., is a nonprofit conservative Mennonite publishing company providing Christ-centered, Biblical literature in a variety of forms including Gospel tracts, books, Sunday school materials, summer Bible school materials, and a full curriculum for Christian day schools and homeschools.

For more information at no obligation or for spiritual help, please write to us at:
    Christian Light Publications, Inc.
    P. O. Box 1212
    Harrisonburg, VA 22801-1212